MW00978283

2dfd3356ae9fe46895e035847859e24e

This is an educational material. Content is based on the author best knowledge to date.

# 100 Phonetics Crosswords

## Homophones

**XOXOMary**

# About the Author

The XOXOMary team wrote this book. XOXOMary is an online platform where you can learn American English. On XOXOMary, we publish new educational material daily. Visit www.xoxomary.com to find crosswords and other material online. We hope this book helps you improve your American English pronunciation. And we wish you have fun solving the puzzles.

# Table of Contents

Introduction                                    5

Crosswords                                      6

Solutions                                     106

Appendix                                      151

# Introduction

This book contains 100 phonetics crosswords. Under each crossword you will find the phonetic transcription of six words. The words selected are homophones. They have the same pronunciation but different meaning and spelling. Your task is to find the word corresponding to the transcription in the crossword. You can check the solutions after the last crossword.

The phonetic transcriptions are in the International Phonetic Alphabet. If you are unfamiliar with IPA sounds, we recommend you to take a look at the Appendix first. There you can find a brief guide that will help you start learning the IPA sounds used in American English.s

# Crossword 1

**Across**
1 naʊ
4 'klæsɪ
6 'hɪlz

**Down**
2 aɪ
3 sɪn
5 ɑrt

# Crossword 2

**Across**

3 'mɔl

5 'praɪd

6 'hɛr

**Down**

1 'fræŋk

2 'brɛd

4 'prɑfət

# Crossword 3

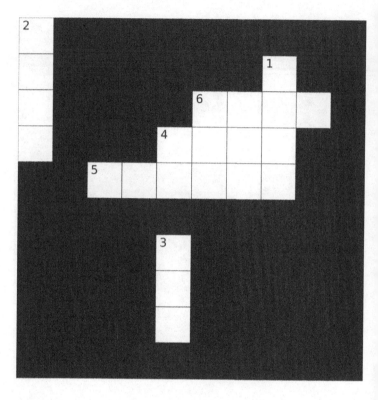

**Across**
4 ʃu
5 'mɪsəl
6 'fli

**Down**
1 pil
2 'tɔt
3 'dʒæm

# Crossword 4

**Across**
2 hɔl
4 'grɪl
6 'reɪz

**Down**
1 weɪd
3 'sɛlər
5 wʌn

# Crossword 5

**Across**
1 'æksəs
3 'kruəl
6 'aʊər

**Down**
2 'klɔz
4 maɪt
5 'kwɔrts

# Crossword 6

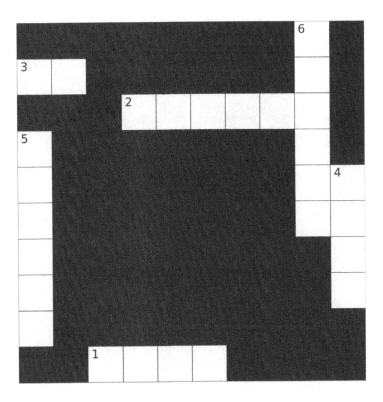

**Across**
1 'peɪn
2 'tækt
3 wi

**Down**
4 'ɛrɪ
5 slaɪt
6 'mɛdəl

# Crossword 7

**Across**
3 'saɪd
5 eɪt
6 'loʊd

**Down**
1 'bɪtʃ
2 kæst
4 'heɪl

# Crossword 8

**Across**
1 'bɛri
2 'mɪst
3 'lɪvɪ

**Down**
4 'tiz
5 'sɪm
6 'laɪ

# Crossword 9

**Across**
3 noʊ
4 'mɛdəl
6 'bruz

**Down**
1 wʊd
2 wik
5 wʊd

# Crossword 10

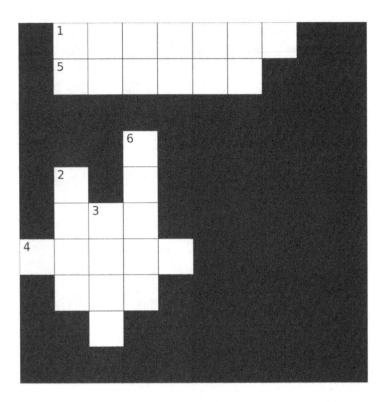

**Across**

1 'mɑrʃəl

4 pis

5 'kruz

**Down**

2 teɪl

3 'lɪvɪ

6 'lɪʧ

# Crossword 11

**Across**
4 'duəl
5 saɪd
6 sʌm

**Down**
1 'fɛr
2 ə'tɛndənts
3 boʊld

# Crossword 12

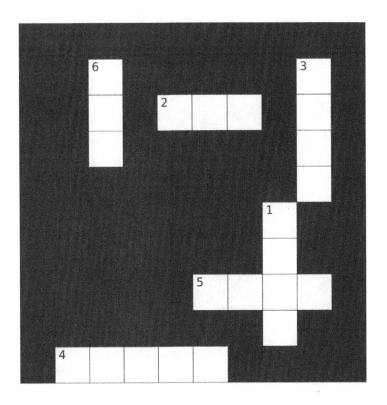

**Across**

2 'leɪ

4 maɪt

5 noʊ

**Down**

1 nɑt

3 'aɪdəl

6 'ti

# Crossword 13

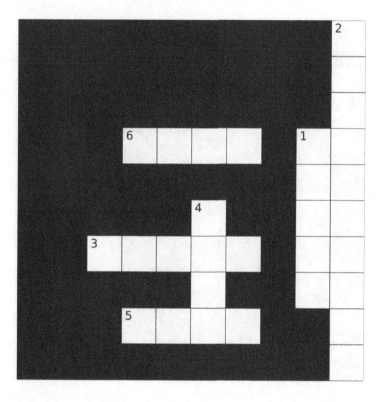

**Across**
3 'gɪld
5 'tiz
6 noʊ

**Down**
1 'rʌŋ
2 'kɑmpləmɛnt
4 'fli

# Crossword 14

**Across**

2 taɪm
3 'boʊ
6 'reɪn

**Down**

1 'pɔz
4 'rɪŋ
5 'rik

# Crossword 15

**Across**
2 'meɪz
4 braɪdəl
6 bʌt

**Down**
1 'ʃut
3 ʃoʊn
5 ɛr

# Crossword 16

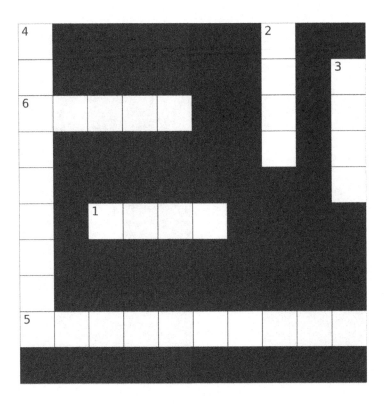

**Across**
1 soʊl
5 ˈsteɪʃənˌɛrɪ
6 ˈklɔz

**Down**
2 noʊz
3 ˈhoʊli
4 ˈɪnsədənts

# Crossword 17

**Across**
3 'sɪ,riəl
4 'mɪst
6 'mʌstərd

**Down**
1 'ɔr
2 'sɛnsər
5 'tɪr

# Crossword 18

**Across**
3 oʊ
5 'soʊl
6 'kruəl

**Down**
1 'fraɪər
2 wʊd
4 'rik

# Crossword 19

**Across**

1 'fɪt

2 hir

4 'loʊd

**Down**

3 'gæf

5 oʊ

6 'veɪl

# Crossword 20

**Across**
1 nɑt
5 loʊn
6 'kju

**Down**
2 baʊ
3 'siz
4 'lin

# Crossword 21

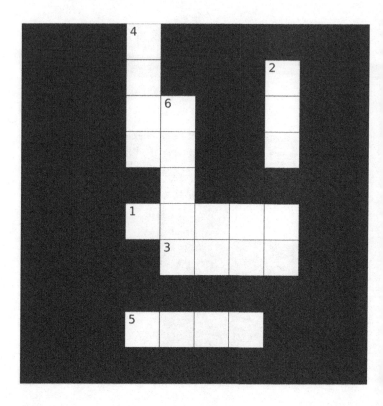

**Across**
1 'neɪvəl
3 roʊd
5 bɪt

**Down**
2 soʊ
4 'oʊd
6 'fraɪər

# Crossword 22

**Across**

2 'duəl

3 'baɪ

5 'pælət

**Down**

1 loʊn

4 æd

6 'dɛnts

# Crossword 23

**Across**
2 'nid
3 'hoʊz
5 'bɔr

**Down**
1 'sɪk
4 bʌt
6 'maɪnər

# Crossword 24

**Across**
2 sɪn
4 'klɔz
6 'lut

**Down**
1 'peɪn
3 'feɪnt
5 'stɛrz

# Crossword 25

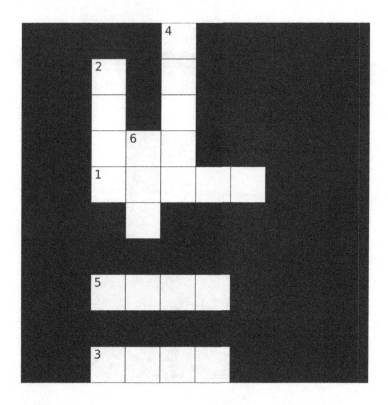

**Across**
1 bɔrd
3 'fli
5 saɪt

**Down**
2 'dʒæm
4 'maɪnər
6 sʌn

# Crossword 26

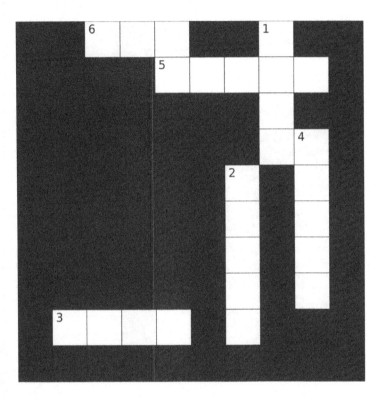

**Across**

3 hɛr
5 'toʊd
6 hɪm

**Down**

1 'siz
2 'pliz
4 'greɪt

# Crossword 27

**Across**
2 tɔt
3 'hil
4 noʊ

**Down**
1 'weɪst
5 'bitʃ
6 'θaɪm

# Crossword 28

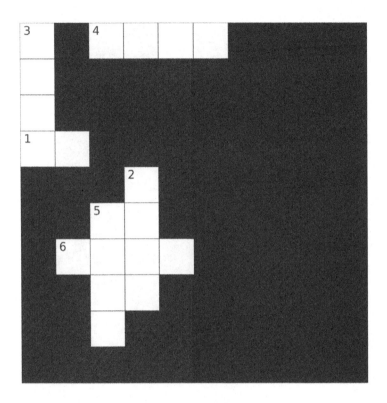

**Across**
1 noʊ
4 'loʊn
6 'faʊl

**Down**
2 'plʌm
3 'wɔrn
5 dʌn

# Crossword 29

**Across**
1 'daɪɪŋ
2 'kɔrs
3 baʊ

**Down**
4 fɔr
5 'tɪk
6 'ʃik

# Crossword 30

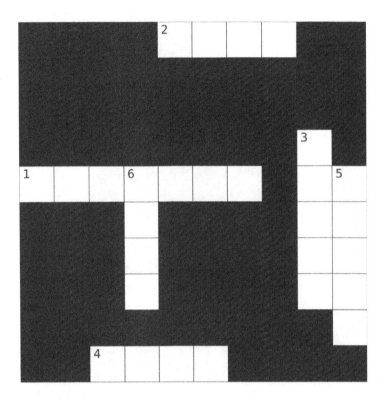

**Across**

1 kloʊðz
2 heɪl
4 sɛl

**Down**

3 'swit
5 'ʃɪr
6 'tim

# Crossword 31

**Across**
1 əˈlaʊd
4 ˈwɛrz
5 boʊld

**Down**
2 ˈbrud
3 ˈfaɪnd
6 pæst

# Crossword 32

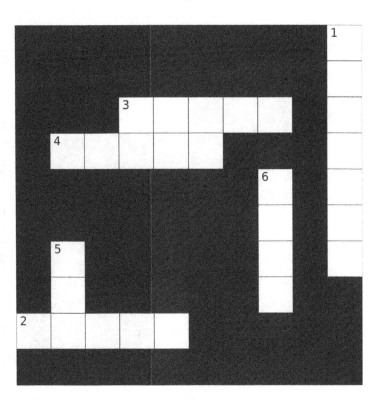

**Across**

2 'praɪz
3 'sɔrd
4 'breɪk

**Down**

1 'silɪŋ
5 ɛr
6 meɪn

# Crossword 33

**Across**
1 'du
2 'æk,siz
6 'lin

**Down**
3 wi
4 'neɪv
5 'pækt

# Crossword 34

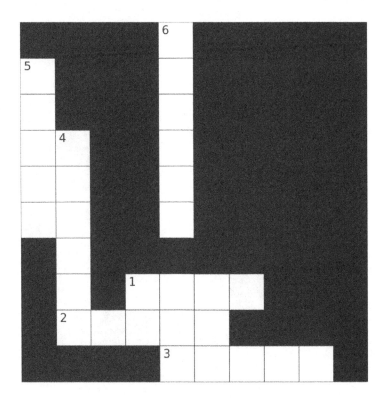

**Across**

1 teɪl
2 'lɪtʃ
3 'ɔltər

**Down**

4 'hɑstəl
5 saɪt
6 'saɪts

# Crossword 35

**Across**
1 faɪnd
4 'bɔld
6 'doʊ

**Down**
2 'taɪd
3 'silɪŋ
5 'mɪst

# Crossword 36

**Across**
4 weɪd
5 wʊd
6 rɛd

**Down**
1 'gæf
2 ən'du
3 'meɪz

# Crossword 37

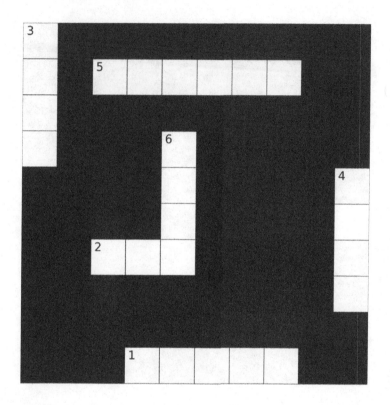

**Across**
1 'flɛr
2 laɪ
5 'praɪmər

**Down**
3 'dʒaɪb
4 'pɔr
6 hoʊl

# Crossword 38

**Across**

1 'roʊz

5 'flɛr

6 'maɪnər

**Down**

2 saɪt

3 bʌt

4 'sɪlɪŋ

# Crossword 39

**Across**
1 'tiz
2 dʌz
6 æd

**Down**
3 pɔr
4 ti
5 'blɑk

# Crossword 40

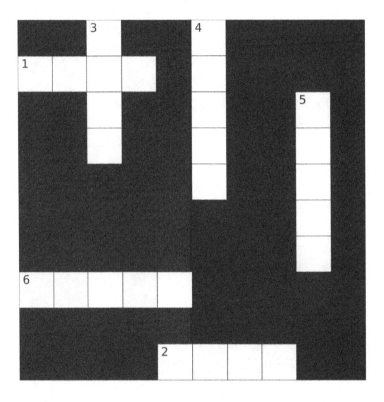

**Across**

1 teɪl
2 'hoʊli
6 pɪs

**Down**

3 saɪd
4 staɪl
5 'gæf

# Crossword 41

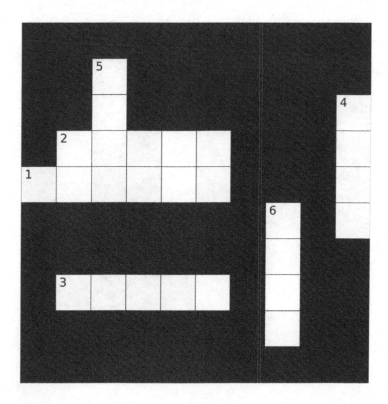

**Across**

1 'sɛnsər

2 'seɪn

3 maɪt

**Down**

4 'hɪm

5 'lin

6 'rɪŋ

# Crossword 42

**Across**

3 tu

5 ˈkɔrəl

6 ˈkɛrət

**Down**

1 ˈboʊldər

2 ˈpraɪz

4 ˈdɪr

# Crossword 43

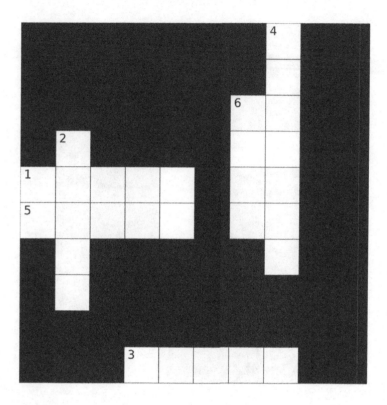

**Across**
1 'weɪ
3 'maɪnd
5 praɪs

**Down**
2 'sɜrdʒ
4 'weɪd
6 weɪt

# Crossword 44

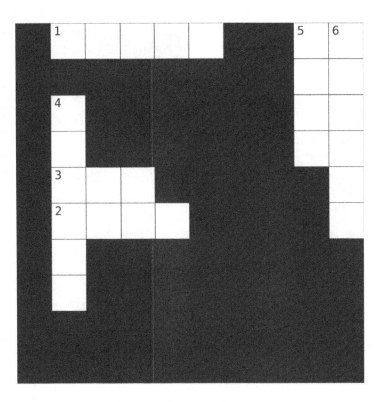

**Across**
1 'plʌm
2 'tækt
3 'sɪk

**Down**
4 'hɑstəl
5 lɪd
6 'kænən

# Crossword 45

**Across**
1 pɪr
2 soʊ
4 'lɪvɪ

**Down**
3 'sɔr
5 'ɔltər
6 'du

# Crossword 46

**Across**
1 'hil
4 'krik
6 'toʊd

**Down**
2 sæk
3 'neɪv
5 'faʊl

# Crossword 47

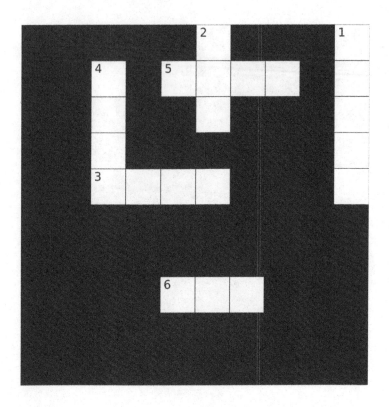

**Across**
3 taɪm
5 'bɑrd
6 'dʒæm

**Down**
1 'mus
2 tæks
4 rɛst

# Crossword 48

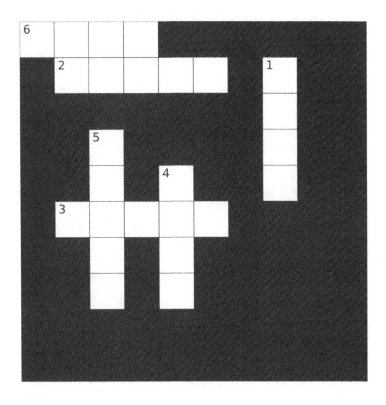

**Across**
2 'nid
3 'neɪvəl
6 'reɪn

**Down**
1 stɛp
4 'bɔld
5 'flɛr

# Crossword 49

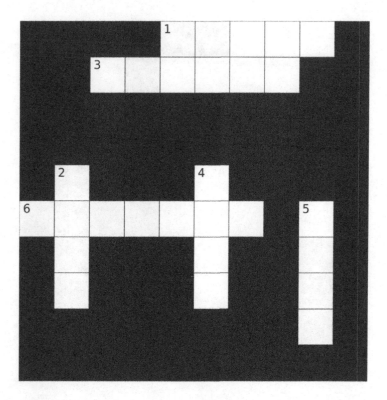

**Across**
1 'grɪl
3 'friz
6 'marʃəl

**Down**
2 meɪn
4 beɪs
5 pɔr

# Crossword 50

**Across**
3 teɪl
5 'daɪɪŋ
6 'dʒinz

**Down**
1 hɜrd
2 'steɪk
4 lɛd

# Crossword 51

**Across**
2 'tɪk
3 'daɪ
4 'roʊt

**Down**
1 'tɪr
5 'joʊk
6 'mɔl

# Crossword 52

**Across**
1 'leɪn
3 'eɪl
6 'lɪvɪ

**Down**
2 raɪt
4 'gaɪz
5 'leɪn

# Crossword 53

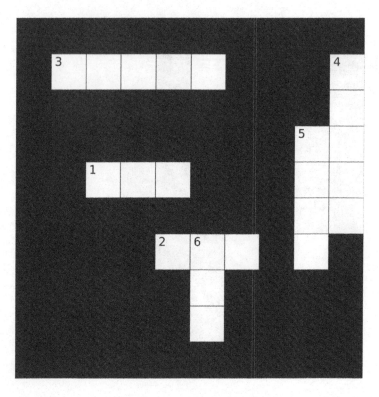

**Across**
1 'fɝr
2 'ɝn
3 'hɔrs

**Down**
4 'læps
5 roʊl
6 rɛd

# Crossword 54

**Across**

4 'wɑn
5 'nɪks
6 weɪ

**Down**

1 bʌt
2 'liʧ
3 'θroʊz

# Crossword 55

**Across**
2 'leɪn
4 'iv
6 laɪ

**Down**
1 'sim
3 'mæntəl
5 pis

# Crossword 56

**Across**
1 'hɑrt
2 'sɛnsər
3 'sæk

**Down**
4 bɔrd
5 'sleɪ
6 'nɪks

# Crossword 57

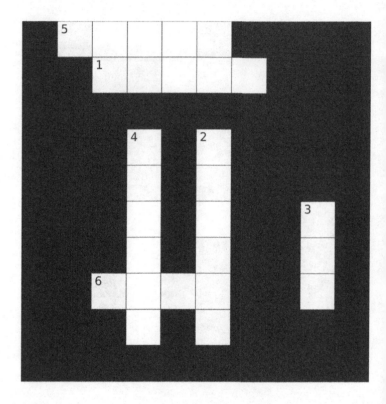

**Across**

1 'hɔrs

5 'plʌm

6 weɪv

**Down**

2 'steɪd

3 sʌn

4 braɪdəl

# Crossword 58

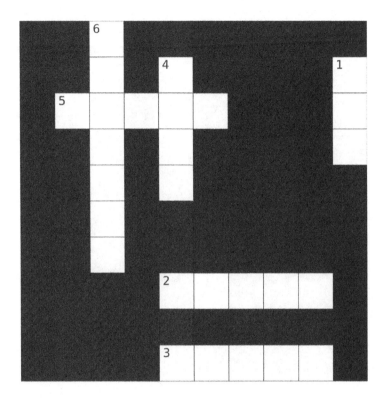

**Across**
2 bɔrd
3 'swit
5 'bruz

**Down**
1 laɪ
4 'oʊd
6 gər'ɪlə

# Crossword 59

**Across**
1 'aʊər
2 'kwaɪər
3 braɪdəl

**Down**
4 'neɪv
5 'kɔrəl
6 'ʤæm

# Crossword 60

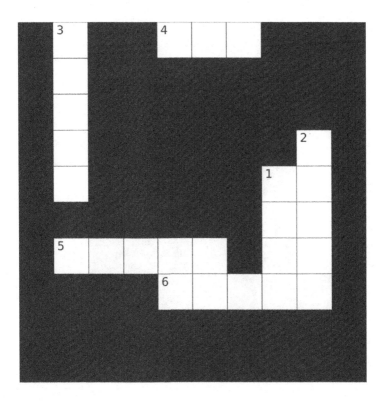

**Across**
4 'hju
5 'sɜrdʒ
6 hoʊl

**Down**
1 'bɔl
2 'peɪst
3 pis

# Crossword 61

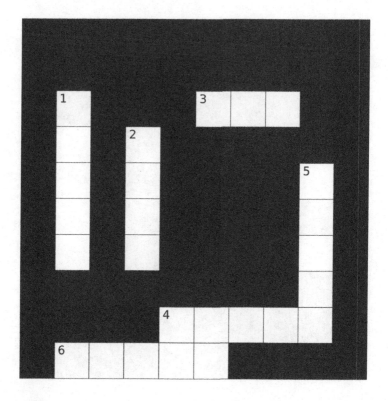

**Across**
3 juz
4 groʊn
6 'faɪnd

**Down**
1 'fraɪər
2 hɛr
5 'groʊn

# Crossword 62

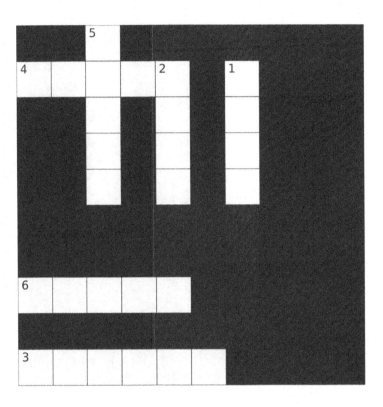

**Across**

3 'boʊld

4 'trækt

6 'faɪnd

**Down**

1 soʊl

2 taɪd

5 'bærən

# Crossword 63

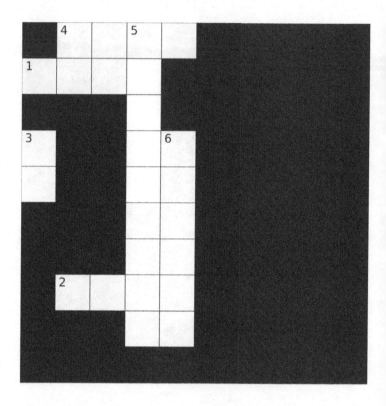

**Across**
1 bɛr
2 'lut
4 'bɛri

**Down**
3 haɪ
5 'rɛzɪdənts
6 'pækt

# Crossword 64

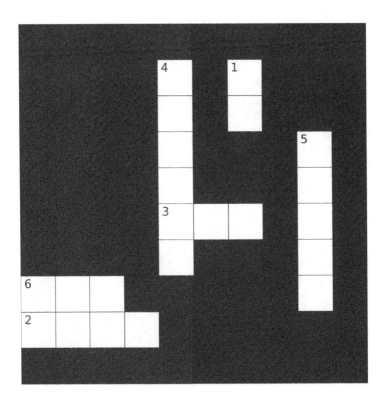

**Across**

2 loʊn

3 aɪ

6 juz

**Down**

1 noʊ

4 'θroʊz

5 'θaɪm

# Crossword 65

**Across**
1 trup
3 'ɜrn
4 stil

**Down**
2 'θroʊz
5 'kwaɪr
6 ðɛr

# Crossword 66

**Across**
1 hɔl
2 'taɪər
3 'fɪʃər

**Down**
4 'kruəl
5 'faɪnd
6 'meɪn

# Crossword 67

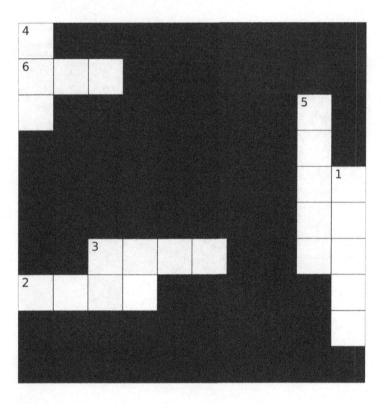

**Across**
2 'ril
3 'geɪt
6 'ɔr

**Down**
1 'bɜrθ
4 'toʊ
5 'weɪ

# Crossword 68

**Across**

2 'tiz

3 'sæk

6 fit

**Down**

1 'kɔrs

4 'tɪk

5 'hɑstəl

# Crossword 69

**Across**

1 kloʊðz

2 trup

5 nid

**Down**

3 'joʊk

4 weɪ

6 'floʊ

# Crossword 70

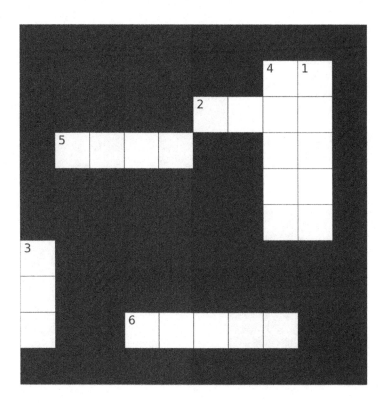

**Across**
2 pil
5 fɔr
6 'roʊd

**Down**
1 'ɔltər
3 'heɪ
4 'lɪtʃ

# Crossword 71

**Across**

1 'pɛdəl
2 'vaɪs
6 'mɪns

**Down**

3 'flaʊər
4 'hoʊz
5 'bɔr

# Crossword 72

**Across**
1 taɪm
2 'kɛrət
3 'sɪm

**Down**
4 meɪd
5 'eɪt
6 baɪ

# Crossword 73

**Across**

3 'bɜrθ
4 'bɛl
6 'breɪk

**Down**

1 'ɑrk
2 'læks
5 groʊn

# Crossword 74

**Across**

1 'geɪt

2 taɪm

3 'kju

**Down**

4 tɜrn

5 'praɪd

6 weɪ

# Crossword 75

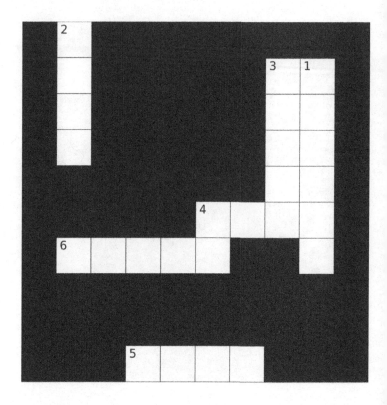

**Across**

4 'hoʊz
5 'lin
6 'tɛnts

**Down**

1 'toʊld
2 roʊd
3 'pliz

# Crossword 76

**Across**

3 'praɪd
4 'prɪnsəpəl
5 roʊl

**Down**

1 'weɪst
2 'fɜr
6 sin

# Crossword 77

**Across**

2 gər'ɪlə

3 ə'sɛnt

5 'pleɪt

**Down**

1 'lɑks

4 'gɔrd

6 bit

# Crossword 78

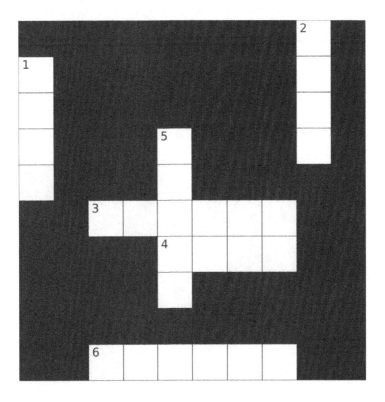

**Across**
3 'kruz
4 'leɪn
6 pliz

**Down**
1 fɛr
2 ʃu
5 'skʌl

# Crossword 79

**Across**
1 sɪn
2 'tɛns
6 dɪs'krɪt

**Down**
3 weɪd
4 'daɪɪŋ
5 'ɜːn

# Crossword 80

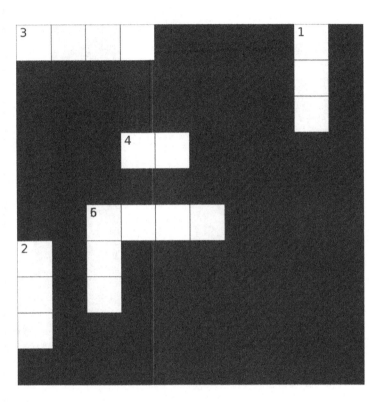

**Across**
3 'boʊ
4 oʊ
6 taɪd

**Down**
1 sʌn
2 'laɪ
5 tu

# Crossword 81

**Across**
3 oʊ
4 ˈkɛrət
6 si

**Down**
1 ˈgɔrd
2 ˈrɪŋ
5 ˈkɔrs

# Crossword 82

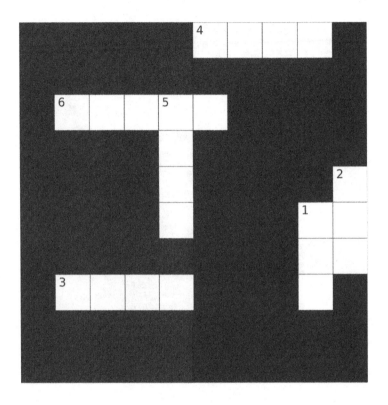

**Across**
3 'veɪn
4 'lɑmə
6 'flɛr

**Down**
1 'fɜr
2 bʌt
5 'rʌŋ

# Crossword 83

**Across**
2 brɛd
3 'faʊl
6 'aɪdəl

**Down**
1 'ʃɪrn
4 ɪn
5 'kænən

# Crossword 84

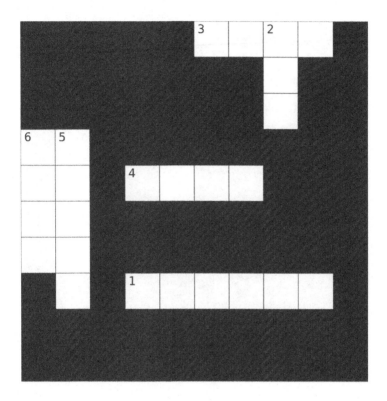

**Across**
1 'hɑstəl
3 'taɪər
4 'veɪn

**Down**
2 'ju
5 noʊz
6 'mɔl

# Crossword 85

**Across**
3 'streɪt
5 'tim
6 'plʌm

**Down**
1 'blɑk
2 'rɪŋ
4 'skʌl

# Crossword 86

**Across**

3 'toʊld
4 'kæləs
5 nɑt

**Down**

1 'mɔl
2 'wɔrn
6 'tækt

# Crossword 87

**Across**
2 'loʊd
3 ə'sɛnt
4 'bɔld

**Down**
1 'ril
5 'ɔltər
6 rut

# Crossword 88

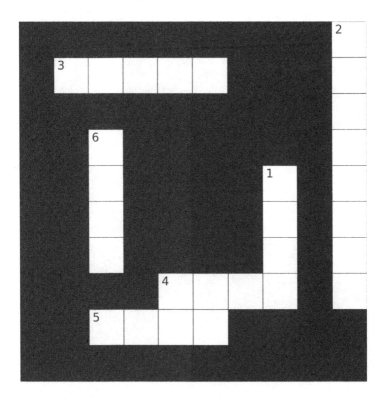

**Across**
3 bɪld
4 floʊ
5 tim

**Down**
1 noʊ
2 ˈprɛzəns
6 ˈæksəs

# Crossword 89

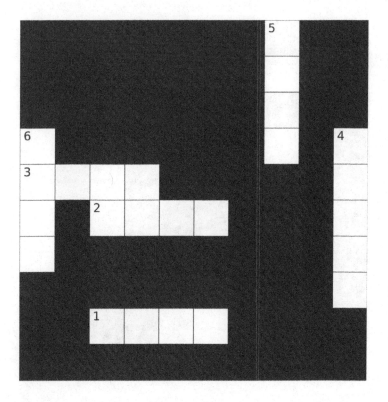

**Across**
1 'boʊ
2 'leɪn
3 'aɪdəl

**Down**
4 'ɔltər
5 'wɔrn
6 'rɪŋ

# Crossword 90

**Across**
2 'ɪnsədəns
5 'bɔr
6 sʌn

**Down**
1 bɔrd
3 'læks
4 'loʊn

# Crossword 91

**Across**
2 'ril
5 hir
6 'mʌsəl

**Down**
1 floʊ
3 'maɪt
4 'stɛp

# Crossword 92

**Across**

1 əˈtɛndəns
3 faɪnd
5 pæst

**Down**

2 ˈrʌŋ
4 ˈlin
6 eɪt

# Crossword 93

**Across**

1 ˈeɪl
2 naɪt
3 ˈswit

**Down**

4 ˈkæpɪtəl
5 ˈsɛlər
6 ˈrʌŋ

# Crossword 94

**Across**
2 weɪst
4 sim
6 bitʃ

**Down**
1 'ʃik
3 'beɪtɪd
5 'kɔrəl

# Crossword 95

**Across**

2 'bɔr
4 'aɪdəl
6 'tɪk

**Down**

1 'kwɔrts
3 'kæpɪtəl
5 'dæm

# Crossword 96

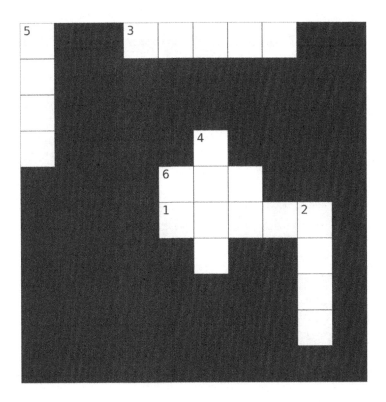

**Across**
1 'skʌl
3 'maɪnər
6 'neɪ

**Down**
2 'loʊd
4 'pækt
5 'veɪl

# Crossword 97

**Across**
1 'hoʊli
3 'tɛns
6 'daɪ

**Down**
2 bɔrd
4 'bɛri
5 'mɪst

# Crossword 98

**Across**

2 weɪt

3 ʃoʊn

6 'θroʊz

**Down**

1 'loʊ

4 'doʊ

5 'sleɪ

# Crossword 99

**Across**
1 'sɪk
2 'grɪl
3 'sɔr

**Down**
4 'lɛsən
5 blu
6 'duəl

# Crossword 100

**Across**
1 wʊd
2 'praɪz
4 'kɛrət

**Down**
3 'meɪn
5 'poʊl
6 'steɪk

# Solutions

## Crossword 1

### Across

- 1 now
- 4 classy
- 6 hills

### Down

- 2 I
- 3 seen
- 5 art

## Crossword 2

### Across

- 3 mall
- 5 pried
- 6 hare

### Down

- 1 frank
- 2 bred
- 4 prophet

# Crossword 3

## Across

- 4 shoe
- 5 missal
- 6 flee

## Down

- 1 peel
- 2 taut
- 3 jam

# Crossword 4

## Across

- 2 haul
- 4 grille
- 6 rays

## Down

- 1 wade
- 3 seller
- 5 one

# Crossword 5

## Across

- 1 axis
- 3 cruel
- 6 our

## Down

- 2 clause
- 4 might
- 5 quarts

# Crossword 6

## Across

- 1 pane
- 2 tacked
- 3 we

## Down

- 4 airy
- 5 slight
- 6 meddle

# Crossword 7

## Across

- 3 sighed

- 5 eight
- 6 load

## Down

- 1 beech
- 2 cast
- 4 hale

# Crossword 8

## Across

- 1 bury
- 2 mist
- 3 levy

## Down

- 4 tease
- 5 seam
- 6 lye

# Crossword 9

## Across

- 3 no
- 4 meddle
- 6 brews

## Down

- 1 wood
- 2 week
- 5 would

# Crossword 10

## Across

- 1 marshal
- 4 piece
- 5 cruise

## Down

- 2 tail
- 3 levy
- 6 leech

# Crossword 11

## Across

- 4 duel
- 5 side
- 6 sum

## Down

- 1 fare
- 2 attendants
- 3 bold

# Crossword 12

## Across

- 2 lei
- 4 might
- 5 know

## Down

- 1 knot
- 3 idle
- 6 tee

# Crossword 13

## Across

- 3 guild
- 5 teas
- 6 know

## Down

- 1 wrung
- 2 compliment
- 4 flea

# Crossword 14

## Across

- 2 time
- 3 beau
- 6 reign

## Down

- 1 pause
- 4 ring
- 5 wreak

# Crossword 15

## Across

- 2 maze
- 4 bridal
- 6 butt

## Down

- 1 chute
- 3 shown
- 5 air

# Crossword 16

## Across

- 1 soul

- 5 stationery
- 6 claws

## Down

- 2 nose
- 3 holy
- 4 incidents

# Crossword 17

## Across

- 3 serial
- 4 mist
- 6 mustered

## Down

- 1 oar
- 2 sensor
- 5 tear

# Crossword 18

## Across

- 3 oh
- 5 sole
- 6 crewel

## Down

- 1 friar
- 2 would
- 4 reek

# Crossword 19

## Across

- 1 feat
- 2 hear
- 4 lode

## Down

- 3 gaff
- 5 oh
- 6 vale

# Crossword 20

## Across

- 1 not
- 5 loan
- 6 queue

## Down

- 2 bow
- 3 seize
- 4 lien

# Crossword 21

## Across

- 1 naval
- 3 road
- 5 beat

## Down

- 2 sow
- 4 owed
- 6 friar

# Crossword 22

## Across

- 2 duel
- 3 bye
- 5 palette

## Down

- 1 loan
- 4 add
- 6 dents

# Crossword 23

## Across

- 2 knead
- 3 hoes
- 5 bore

## Down

- 1 sick
- 4 butt
- 6 minor

# Crossword 24

## Across

- 2 scene
- 4 claws
- 6 loot

## Down

- 1 pane
- 3 feint
- 5 stares

# Crossword 25

## Across

- 1 bored

- 3 flee
- 5 cite

## Down

- 2 jamb
- 4 minor
- 6 son

# Crossword 26

## Across

- 3 hair
- 5 towed
- 6 him

## Down

- 1 seas
- 2 pleas
- 4 grate

# Crossword 27

## Across

- 2 taught
- 3 heel
- 4 no

## Down

- 1 waist
- 5 beech
- 6 thyme

# Crossword 28

## Across

- 1 no
- 4 lone
- 6 foul

## Down

- 2 plum
- 3 worn
- 5 done

# Crossword 29

## Across

- 1 dying
- 2 coarse
- 3 bow

## Down

- 4 for
- 5 tick
- 6 sheik

# Crossword 30

## Across

- 1 clothes
- 2 hail
- 4 sell

## Down

- 3 sweet
- 5 sheer
- 6 teem

# Crossword 31

## Across

- 1 aloud
- 4 wares
- 5 bold

## Down

- 2 brood
- 3 fined
- 6 passed

# Crossword 32

## Across

- 2 pries
- 3 sword
- 4 break

## Down

- 1 ceiling
- 5 air
- 6 main

# Crossword 33

## Across

- 1 due
- 2 axes
- 6 lien

## Down

- 3 we
- 4 nave
- 5 pact

# Crossword 34

## Across

- 1 tail

- 2 leach
- 3 alter

## Down

- 4 hostel
- 5 sight
- 6 sights

# Crossword 35

## Across

- 1 find
- 4 bald
- 6 doe

## Down

- 2 tide
- 3 ceiling
- 5 missed

# Crossword 36

## Across

- 4 wade
- 5 would
- 6 red

## Down

- 1 gaff
- 2 undue
- 3 maize

# Crossword 37

## Across

- 1 flair
- 2 lie
- 5 primer

## Down

- 3 jibe
- 4 pore
- 6 hole

# Crossword 38

## Across

- 1 rows
- 5 flair
- 6 miner

## Down

- 2 sight
- 3 butt
- 4 sealing

# Crossword 39

## Across

- 1 teas
- 2 does
- 6 ad

## Down

- 3 pour
- 4 tea
- 5 block

# Crossword 40

## Across

- 1 tail
- 2 holy
- 6 piece

## Down

- 3 side
- 4 style
- 5 gaffe

# Crossword 41

## Across

- 1 sensor
- 2 seine
- 3 might

## Down

- 4 hymn
- 5 lien
- 6 ring

# Crossword 42

## Across

- 3 too
- 5 choral
- 6 carat

## Down

- 1 bolder
- 2 prize
- 4 dear

# Crossword 43

## Across

- 1 weigh

- 3 mined
- 5 price

## Down

- 2 serge
- 4 weighed
- 6 wait

# Crossword 44

## Across

- 1 plumb
- 2 tact
- 3 sic

## Down

- 4 hostel
- 5 lead
- 6 cannon

# Crossword 45

## Across

- 1 peer
- 2 sow
- 4 levy

## Down

- 3 soar
- 5 alter
- 6 due

# Crossword 46

## Across

- 1 heel
- 4 creak
- 6 toad

## Down

- 2 sack
- 3 nave
- 5 fowl

# Crossword 47

## Across

- 3 time
- 5 bard
- 6 jam

## Down

- 1 moose
- 2 tax
- 4 rest

# Crossword 48

## Across

- 2 knead
- 3 naval
- 6 rain

## Down

- 1 step
- 4 bald
- 5 flair

# Crossword 49

## Across

- 1 grill
- 3 frieze
- 6 marshal

## Down

- 2 main
- 4 bass
- 5 pour

# Crossword 50

## Across

- 3 tale
- 5 dyeing
- 6 jeans

## Down

- 1 heard
- 2 steak
- 4 led

# Crossword 51

## Across

- 2 tick
- 3 dye
- 4 rote

## Down

- 1 tear
- 5 yoke
- 6 mall

# Crossword 52

## Across

- 1 lane

- 3 ail
- 6 levy

## Down

- 2 right
- 4 guys
- 5 lain

# Crossword 53

## Across

- 1 fir
- 2 urn
- 3 horse

## Down

- 4 lapse
- 5 roll
- 6 red

# Crossword 54

## Across

- 4 won
- 5 nicks
- 6 way

## Down

- 1 but
- 2 leach
- 3 throes

# Crossword 55

## Across

- 2 lain
- 4 eve
- 6 lie

## Down

- 1 seam
- 3 mantel
- 5 piece

# Crossword 56

## Across

- 1 hart
- 2 censor
- 3 sac

## Down

- 4 board
- 5 slay
- 6 nicks

# Crossword 57

## Across

- 1 horse
- 5 plumb
- 6 wave

## Down

- 2 stayed
- 3 son
- 4 bridal

# Crossword 58

## Across

- 2 bored
- 3 sweet
- 5 brews

## Down

- 1 lie
- 4 owed
- 6 gorilla

# Crossword 59

## Across

- 1 our
- 2 choir
- 3 bridle

## Down

- 4 nave
- 5 choral
- 6 jamb

# Crossword 60

## Across

- 4 hew
- 5 serge
- 6 whole

## Down

- 1 bawl
- 2 paste
- 3 peace

# Crossword 61

## Across

- 3 use

- 4 grown
- 6 fined

## Down

- 1 friar
- 2 hair
- 5 groan

# Crossword 62

## Across

- 3 bowled
- 4 tract
- 6 fined

## Down

- 1 soul
- 2 tied
- 5 baron

# Crossword 63

## Across

- 1 bare
- 2 lute
- 4 bury

## Down

- 3 hi
- 5 residents
- 6 packed

# Crossword 64

## Across

- 2 loan
- 3 eye
- 6 use

## Down

- 1 no
- 4 throes
- 5 thyme

# Crossword 65

## Across

- 1 troop
- 3 urn
- 4 steal

## Down

- 2 throws
- 5 quire
- 6 their

# Crossword 66

## Across

- 1 haul
- 2 tier
- 3 fissure

## Down

- 4 crewel
- 5 fined
- 6 mane

# Crossword 67

## Across

- 2 reel
- 3 gait
- 6 ore

## Down

- 1 birth
- 4 toe
- 5 weigh

# Crossword 68

## Across

- 2 tease
- 3 sac
- 6 feet

## Down

- 1 coarse
- 4 tic
- 5 hostel

# Crossword 69

## Across

- 1 clothes
- 2 troop
- 5 need

## Down

- 3 yoke
- 4 way
- 6 floe

# Crossword 70

## Across

- 2 peel

- 5 four
- 6 rowed

## Down

- 1 alter
- 3 hay
- 4 leech

# Crossword 71

## Across

- 1 peddle
- 2 vise
- 6 mince

## Down

- 3 flower
- 4 hose
- 5 boar

# Crossword 72

## Across

- 1 time
- 2 carrot
- 3 seam

## Down

- 4 made
- 5 ate
- 6 buy

# Crossword 73

## Across

- 3 birth
- 4 bell
- 6 break

## Down

- 1 ark
- 2 lax
- 5 grown

# Crossword 74

## Across

- 1 gait
- 2 time
- 3 queue

## Down

- 4 turn
- 5 pried
- 6 way

# Crossword 75

## Across

- 4 hose
- 5 lien
- 6 tents

## Down

- 1 tolled
- 2 road
- 3 pleas

# Crossword 76

## Across

- 3 pride
- 4 principle
- 5 roll

## Down

- 1 waist
- 2 fur
- 6 scene

# Crossword 77

## Across

- 2 gorilla
- 3 assent
- 5 plait

## Down

- 1 lox
- 4 gored
- 6 beat

# Crossword 78

## Across

- 3 cruise
- 4 lain
- 6 please

## Down

- 1 fair
- 2 shoe
- 5 skull

# Crossword 79

## Across

- 1 scene

- 2 tense
- 6 discreet

## Down

- 3 wade
- 4 dying
- 5 urn

# Crossword 80

## Across

- 3 beau
- 4 oh
- 6 tied

## Down

- 1 son
- 2 lye
- 5 too

# Crossword 81

## Across

- 3 oh
- 4 carat
- 6 see

## Down

- 1 gored
- 2 ring
- 5 coarse

# Crossword 82

## Across

- 3 vain
- 4 lama
- 6 flare

## Down

- 1 fir
- 2 but
- 5 rung

# Crossword 83

## Across

- 2 bread
- 3 fowl
- 6 idle

## Down

- 1 shearn
- 4 in
- 5 cannon

# Crossword 84

## Across

- 1 hostel
- 3 tier
- 4 vein

## Down

- 2 ewe
- 5 knows
- 6 mall

# Crossword 85

## Across

- 3 strait
- 5 teem
- 6 plumb

## Down

- 1 bloc
- 2 wring
- 4 scull

# Crossword 86

## Across

- 3 tolled
- 4 callus
- 5 knot

## Down

- 1 mall
- 2 worn
- 6 tacked

# Crossword 87

## Across

- 2 load
- 3 assent
- 4 bald

## Down

- 1 reel
- 5 altar
- 6 root

# Crossword 88

## Across

- 3 build

- 4 flow
- 5 team

## Down

- 1 know
- 2 presence
- 6 axis

# Crossword 89

## Across

- 1 beau
- 2 lain
- 3 idle

## Down

- 4 alter
- 5 worn
- 6 ring

# Crossword 90

## Across

- 2 incidence
- 5 boar
- 6 son

## Down

- 1 bored
- 3 lax
- 4 lone

# Crossword 91

## Across

- 2 reel
- 5 hear
- 6 muscle

## Down

- 1 flow
- 3 mite
- 4 steppe

# Crossword 92

## Across

- 1 attendance
- 3 find
- 5 past

## Down

- 2 rung
- 4 lien
- 6 eight

# Crossword 93

## Across

- 1 ail
- 2 night
- 3 suite

## Down

- 4 capitol
- 5 seller
- 6 wrung

# Crossword 94

## Across

- 2 waste
- 4 seem
- 6 beach

## Down

- 1 chic
- 3 bated
- 5 coral

# Crossword 95

## Across

- 2 boar
- 4 idle
- 6 tick

## Down

- 1 quarts
- 3 capitol
- 5 damn

# Crossword 96

## Across

- 1 scull
- 3 minor
- 6 nay

## Down

- 2 load
- 4 pact
- 5 veil

# Crossword 97

## Across

- 1 holy

- 3 tense
- 6 dye

## Down

- 2 bored
- 4 bury
- 5 missed

# Crossword 98

## Across

- 2 wait
- 3 shown
- 6 throes

## Down

- 1 lo
- 4 dough
- 5 slay

# Crossword 99

## Across

- 1 sic
- 2 grill
- 3 sore

## Down

- 4 lessen
- 5 blue
- 6 duel

# Crossword 100

## Across

- 1 would
- 2 pries
- 4 carat

## Down

- 3 mane
- 5 pole
- 6 stake

# Appendix

## Learn the IPA sounds to improve your speaking skills

Non-native English speakers often experience misunderstandings when talking to Americans. This happens when non-native English speakers pronounce words as they do in the mother tongue. Thus, Americans have problems to understand their accent.

The IPA transcription of a word contains the sounds you need to pronounce English words in the right way. Each of the IPA sounds has its unique graphic representation or symbol. Learning the pronunciation of the symbols will help you communicate better. Yet, it always takes practice, time, and perseverance to develop new skills. You need to coordinate the mouth, tongue, and airflow in ways you have not done before. Thus, we next include a brief guide to help you start learning the consonant and vowel sounds.

## Consonant Sounds

### /dʒ/

- Tongue: The tongue raises. It touches the roof of the mouth. Then it presses the roof of the mouth. Finally, it releases.

- Lips: The corners of the lips are in. The rest of the lips flare.
- Teeth: The teeth are together.
- Air: The air passes through the vocal cords and makes the sound. The air builds up when tongue presses the roof of the mouth. The air comes through when the tongue releases.
- Vocal chords: The vocal chords vibrate.

## /ʧ/

- Tongue: The tongue raises. It touches the roof of the mouth. Then it presses the roof of the mouth. Finally, it releases.
- Lips: The corners of the lips are in. The rest of the lips flare.
- Teeth: The teeth are together.
- Air: The air passes through the mouth. The air builds up when tongue presses the roof of the mouth. The air comes through when the tongue releases.
- Vocal chords: The vocal chords do not vibrate.

## /ʃ/

- Tongue: The tongue raises a bit in the middle. It does not touch the roof of the mouth. It presses against the inside corner of the top teeth. The front part of the tongue comes down not touching anything in the mouth.
- Lips: The corners of the lips are in. The rest of the lips flare.

- Teeth: The teeth are together.
- Air: Air passes through the mouth.
- Vocal chords: The vocal chords do not vibrate.

# /t/

- Tongue: The tongue will come up. The front part will touch the roof of the mouth behind the top teeth. Then it will pull down to release the air.
- Teeth: The teeth are together. Then they separate.
- Air: Air passes through the mouth. First, the air stops. Then, it flows.
- Vocal chords: The vocal chords do not vibrate.

# /ŋ/

- Tongue: The back part of the tongue reaches up and touches the soft palate. The front part of the tongue touches the bottom front teeth.
- Lips: There is a separation between the lips.
- Teeth: There is a separation between the teeth.
- Air: Air passes through the vocal cords to make the sound.
- Vocal chords: The vocal chords vibrate.

# /l/

- Tongue: The tongue is against the back of the upper teeth.
- Air: The air flows around the sides of the mouth.
- Vocal chords: The vocal chords vibrate.

# /f/

- Lips: The bottom lips are in contact with the teeth.
- Teeth: The top teeth press the bottom lips.
- Air: The air flows through the teeth.
- Vocal chords: The vocal chords do not vibrate.

# /n/

- Tongue: Your tongue is against the ridge behind the top teeth.
- Air: The air flows through the nose.
- Vocal chords: The vocal chords vibrate.

# /d/

- Tongue: The tongue comes up. The front part touches the roof of the mouth behind the top teeth. Then it pulls down to release the air.
- Teeth: The teeth are together. Then they separate.
- Air: First, the air stops. Then it flows.
- Vocal chords: The vocal chords vibrate.

# /b/

- Lips: The lips start together. Then they separate.
- Teeth: There is a small gap between the teeth.
- Air: First, the air stops. Then, it flows.
- Vocal chords: The vocal chords vibrate.

# /ð/

- Tongue: The tip of the tongue comes through the teeth.
- Jaw: The jaw and the mouth remain relaxed.
- Vocal chords: The vocal chords vibrate.

# /k/

- Tongue: The back part of the tongue reaches up and touches the soft palate, cutting off the air. The tongue pulls away and the air flows.
- Lips: The lips position to adjust the sound that comes next.
- Air: Air passes through the mouth. First, the air stops. Then, it flows.
- Vocal chords: The vocal chords do not vibrate.

# /r/

- Tongue: The tongue forms an arch near the roof of the mouth. It does not touch any part of the mouth.
- Air: The air flows through a narrow space in your mouth.
- Vocal chords: The vocal chords vibrate.

# /s/

- Tongue: The tongue is behind the teeth.

- Lips:
- Teeth: The teeth remain clenched.
- Air: The air flows through the tip of the tongue towards the edge of the teeth.
- Vocal chords: The vocal chords do not vibrate.

# /p/

- Lips: The lips start together. Then they separate.
- Teeth: There is a separation between the teeth.
- Air: Air passes through the mouth. First, the air stops. Then, it flows.
- Vocal chords: The vocal chords do not vibrate.

# /m/

- Lips: The lips are together.
- Air: The air comes out of the nose. There is no flow of air through the mouth.
- Vocal chords: The vocal chords vibrate.

# /w/

- Tongue: The back of the tongue reaches up high in the back. It does not touch the soft palate. The front part of the tongue remains forward. It touches the bottom front teeth.
- Lips: The lips form a rounded shape. They move away from the face.
- Vocal chords: The vocal chords vibrate.

# /g/

- Tongue: The back part of the tongue reaches up and touches the soft palate, cutting off the air. The tongue pulls away and the air flows.
- Lips: The lips position depends on the sound that comes next.
- Air: First, the air stops. Then it flows.
- Vocal chords: The vocal chords vibrate.

# /θ/

- Tongue: The tip of the tongue comes through the teeth.
- Jaw: The jaw and the mouth relax.
- Air: Air passes through the mouth.
- Vocal chords: The vocal chords do not vibrate.

# /v/

- Lips: The bottom lips are in contact with the teeth.
- Teeth: The top teeth press the bottom lips.
- Vocal chords: The vocal chords vibrate.

# /j/

- Tongue: The mid and front part of the tongue raises and presses against the roof of the mouth. The tip of the tongue comes down and touches

behind the bottom front teeth.
- Air: The throat compresses the airflow.
- Vocal chords: The vocal chords vibrate.

## /z/

- Tongue: The tongue is behind the teeth.
- Teeth: The teeth remain clenched.
- Air: The air flows through the tip of the tongue.
- Vocal chords: The vocal chords vibrate.

## /h/

- Tongue: The position of the tongue depends on the sound that comes next.
- Lips: The lips are open to let the air go through.
- Teeth: There is a separation between the teeth.
- Air: Air passes through the mouth.
- Vocal chords: The vocal chords do not vibrate.

## /ʒ/

- Tongue: The tongue raises a bit in the middle. It does not touch the roof of the mouth. It presses against the inside corner of the top teeth. The front part of the tongue comes down not touching anything in the mouth.
- Lips: The corners of the lips are in. The rest of the lips flare.
- Teeth: The teeth are together.
- Vocal chords: The vocal chords vibrate.

# Vowel Sounds

## /æ/

- Tongue: The tongue is wide. The front stays forward, touching the back of the bottom front teeth. The back part of the tongue stretches up.
- Jaw: The jaw drops.
- Vocal chords: The vocal chords vibrate.

## /i/

- Tongue: The tongue is tense and raises high. Then it moves to the front of the mouth. The tip of the tongue is low and behind the bottom front teeth.
- Lips: The lips are tense and wide.
- Jaw: The jaw drops, opening the mouth a little.
- Vocal chords: The vocal chords vibrate.

## /ɑ/

- Tongue: The tongue is flat and low in the mouth. The tongue is in the center of the mouth. The tip of the tongue touches the back of the bottom front teeth.
- Lips: The lips remain relaxed in a neutral position.
- Jaw: The jaw drops, opening the mouth as wide as possible.

- Vocal chords: The vocal chords vibrate.

# /ə/

- Tongue: The tongue remains forward and relaxed.
- Lips: The lips relax.
- Jaw: The jaw drops.
- Vocal chords: The vocal chords vibrate.

# /ɪ/

- Tongue: The tongue raises high in the mouth. It moves to the front of the mouth. Then the tip of the tongue moves behind the bottom front teeth. The tongue remains relaxed in the front of the mouth.
- Lips: The lips separated and relaxed.
- Jaw: The jaw drops and the mouth opens a little bit.
- Vocal chords: The vocal chords vibrate.

# /ɛ/

- Tongue: The tongue tip touches the back of the bottom front teeth. The middle part of the tongue arches up towards the roof of the mouth.
- Jaw: The jaw drops.
- Vocal chords: The vocal chords vibrate.

# /u/

- Tongue: The back part of the tongue stretches up towards the soft palate. The front part of the tongue remains down, touching, or behind, the bottom front teeth.
- Lips: The lips relax while forming a rounded shape.
- Vocal chords: The vocal chords vibrate.

# /o/

- Tongue: The back of the tongue raises above the middle of the mouth.
- Vocal chords: The vocal chords vibrate.

# /ʊ/

- Tongue: The back of the tongue lifts towards the back of the roof of the mouth.
- Lips: The lips flare.
- Vocal chords: The vocal chords vibrate.

# /a/

- Tongue: The tip of the tongue moves at the bottom of the mouth near the center.
- Jaw: The jaw drops opening the mouth.
- Vocal chords: The vocal chords vibrate.

# /ʌ/

- Tongue: The tongue relaxes. The back of the

tongue presses down a little bit. The tip of the tongue is forward.

- Lips: The lips relax.
- Jaw: The jaw drops.
- Vocal chords: The vocal chords vibrate.

# /ɔ/

- Tongue: The tongue is flat. Then it moves low in the mouth and pulls back. The tip of the tongue should touch the back of the bottom front teeth.
- Lips: The lips form a rounded shape.
- Jaw: The jaw opens and the mouth widens.
- Vocal chords: The vocal chords vibrate.

# /ɜ/

- Tongue: The middle part of the tongue lifts towards the roof of the mouth in the middle. The front of the tongue hangs down. But it does not touch anything.
- Lips: The corners of the lips come in, pushing the lips away from the face.
- Vocal chords: The vocal chords vibrate.

# /e/

- Tongue: The tongue is high at the front of the mouth. It is not at the top of the mouth.
- Lips: The lips are smiling.
- Jaw: The jaw drops, opening the mouth a little bit.

- Vocal chords: The vocal chords vibrate.

Made in the USA
Las Vegas, NV
03 July 2024